I Try
& 10 more chart hits
for Keyboard

Production: Ulf Klenfeldt

Published 2000

International **MUSIC** Publications

International Music Publications Limited
Griffin House 161 Hammersmith Road London W6 8BS England

Music arranged and processed by *Barnes Music Engraving Ltd.*, East Sussex TN22 4HA
Printed by The Panda Group · Haverhill · Suffolk CB9 8PR · UK · Binding by Haverhill Print Finishers

Flying Without Wings

Words and Music by Steve Mac and Wayne Hector

Suggested Registration: Flute / Pop Organ
Rhythm: 8 Beat
Tempo: ♩ = 72

I Try

Words and Music by Macy Gray, Dave Wilder, Jinsoo Lim and Jeremy Ruzumna

Suggested Registration: Electric Piano / Jazz Guitar
Rhythm: 8 Beat
Tempo: ♩ = 76

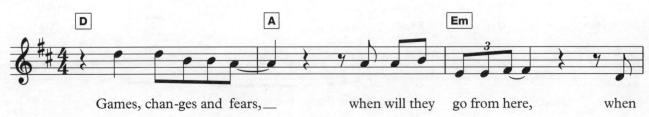

Games, chan-ges and fears,___ when will they go from here, when

will they stop! I be-lieve that fate___ has brought us here___ and we should be to -

- ge-ther babe, but we're___ not. I play it off, but I'm dream-

- ing of you.__ And I'll keep my cool but I'm fiend - ing.__ I try to say good-

- bye and I choke, I try to walk a - way and I stum-ble.Though I try to hide it, it's clear, my world

If You Had My Love

Words and Music by Rodney Jerkins, Lashawn Daniels, Fred Jerkins, Corey Rooney and Jennifer Lopez

Suggested Registration: Brass
Rhythm: Disco
Tempo: ♩ = 110

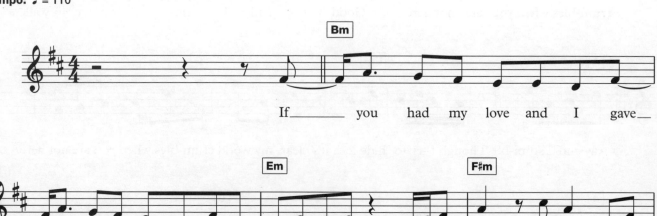

If_____ you had my love and I gave_

_ you all my trust would you com - fort_ me? Tell_ me, ba - by. And if_

_ some - how you knew that your love_____ would be un - true would you lie_

_ to_ me and call me_____ ba - by? Now if I give you me, this is how it's got to

be:_ First of all, I won't take you cheat-ing on_ me._____ Tell me who can I

trust if I can't trust in you? And I re-fuse to let you play me for a

Love's Got A Hold On My Heart

Words and Music by Andrew Frampton and Peter Waterman

Suggested Registration: Pop Organ
Rhythm: Disco or 8 Beat
Tempo: ♩ = 125

(Love's got_ a hold on_ my_ heart.) I'm call - ing out,

_ won't some-bo-dy out there hear my S._ O._ S.?_

Throw me a life - line please an' save_ me. There's no doubt,

_ ba - by you took me pris - 'ner I_ con - fess,_ when you

NORTHERN STAR

Words and Music by Melanie Chisholm and Rick Nowels

Suggested Registration: Electric Guitar
Rhythm: 8 Beat
Tempo: ♩ = 104

They tried to catch a fall-ing_____ star_____

think-ing that she had gone too far._____ She did, but kept it hid-den

well, un-til she cracked and then she___ fell. If all the his-to-ry is___

___ true,_____ she's gon-na end up just like you._____

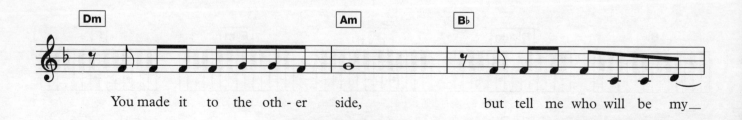

You made it to the oth-er side, but tell me who will be my___

Pure Shores

Words and Music by William Orbit and Shaznay Lewis

Suggested Registration: Flute
Rhythm: 8 Beat (8 Beat Funk)
Tempo: ♩ = 112

I've crossed de - serts for miles, ___ swam wa - ter for a time,

___ search-in' pla - ces to find ___ a piece of some-thing to call ___ mine.

A piece of some-thing to call ___ mine.   (Com-ing clo - ser to you.)

___ Went a - long ___ ma - ny moors ___ walked through ma - ny doors,

___ the place where I wan - na be ___ is the place I can call ___ mine,

SHE

Words and Music by Charles Aznavour and Herbert Kretzmer

Suggested Registration: Vibraphone / Guitar
Rhythm: Swing
Tempo: ♩ = 70

She_may be the face I can't for - get, a trace of plea-sure or re -

- gret, may be my trea-sure or the price I have to pay. She_ may be the song the sum-mer

sings, may be the chill the au-tumn brings, may be a hun-dred dif-ferent

things with-in the mea-sure of a day. She_may be the beau-ty or the

beast, may be the fa-mine or the feast, may turn each day in-to a hea-ven or a hell.

She may be the mir-ror of my dreams, a smile re-flec-ted in a stream, she may not be what she may

seem in-side her shell. She_ who al-ways seems so hap-py in a

crowd, whose eyes can be so pri-vate and so proud, no one's al-lowed to see them when they cry.

She may be the love that can-not hope to last, may come to me from sha-dows of the

past that I'll re-mem-ber till the day I die. She__ may be the rea-son I sur -

- vive the why and where-fore I'm a - live, the one I'll care for through the

rough and rea-dy years. Me,__ I'll take her laugh-ter and her tears, and make them all my sou-ve -

- nirs, for where she goes I've got to be, the mean-ing of my life is she, she, she, oh,_ she.

Sweet Love 2K

Words and Music by Gary Bias, Louis Johnson and Anita Baker

Suggested Registration: Electric Guitar / Strings
Rhythm: Latin Funk or Pop Latin
Tempo: ♩ = 100

With all my heart_ I love_ you ba - by.

Stay with me_ and you will see_ my_ arms_ will hold_ you ba - by.

Nev-er leave coz I be - lieve_ I'm in love._ Sweet love._ Hear me call-

- ing out your name._ I feel_ no shame. I'm in love._ Sweet love.

Don't you ev - er go a - way,_ it-'ll al-ways be this way. There's no

strong - er love_ in this world._ Ah, but I know

Unpretty

Words and Music by Dallas L Austin and Tionne Tenese Watkins

Suggested Registration: Piano / Jazz Guitar
Rhythm: 16 Beat
Tempo: ♩ = 100

I wish I could tie you up in my shoes, make you feel un-pret-ty, too.

I was told I was beau-ti-ful.___ What does that mean to you?___

___ Look in-to the mir-ror. Who's in-side___ there? The one with the long_ hair.___

___ Same old me a-gain to-day,___ yeah.___ My out-sides look cool. My in-

-sides look blue. Ev-'ry-time I think I'm through it's be-cause of you.___ I try

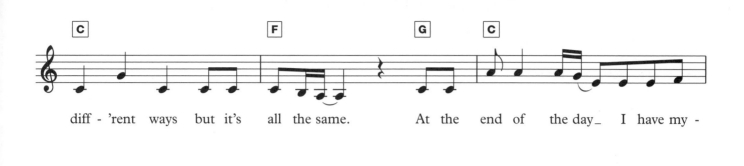

diff - 'rent ways but it's all the same. At the end of the day_ I have my -

- self to blame. I'm just trip-pin'._____ You can buy your hair if it won't grow.

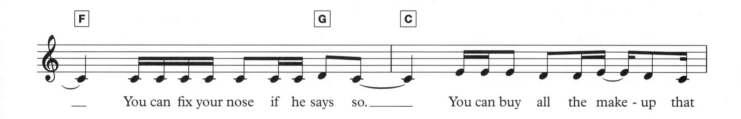

— You can fix your nose if he says so._____ You can buy all the make - up that

man can make. But if____ you can't look in-side you,__ find out who am I, too.

— Be in the po-si-tion to make me feel so damn un-pret-ty._____

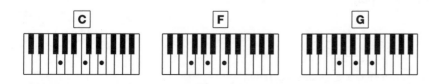

When We Are Together

Words and Music by John McElhone and Sharleen Spiteri

Suggested Registration: Brass
Rhythm: Disco
Tempo: ♩ = 120

Oh I re-mem-ber you said can I fight and breathe. So now I

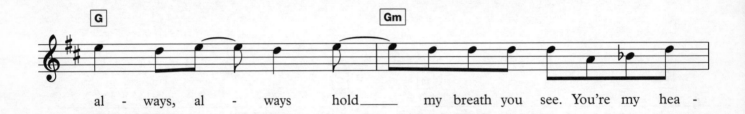

al - ways, al - ways hold___ my breath you see. You're my hea -

- ven, you're my space-man in your shi - ny, shi - ny suit.___ I'll send up

all my prayers and hope they're un-der-stood. Love_ start-ed mak-ing sense.

I al-ways make mis-takes at my ex - pense. Love_ has_ placed a seed,

When You Say Nothing At All

Words and Music by Paul Overstreet and Don Schlitz

Suggested Registration: Flute / Strings
Rhythm: 8 Beat
Tempo: ♩ = 88

It's a - maz - ing how you can speak right to my heart,_

with-out say - ing a word you can light up the dark._____

Try as I may I can nev - er ex - plain_ what I hear_ when you don't

_ say a thing. The smile on your face lets me know

__ that you need me. There's a truth in your eyes say-ing you'll_ nev-er leave me. The

touch of your hand says you'll touch_ me when-ev-er I fall.___

You say it best when you say no-thing at all.___

You say it best when you say no-thing at all.___

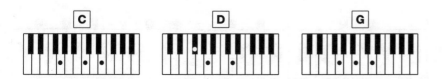

THE EASY KEYBOARD LIBRARY

Also available in the series

THE TWENTIES
including:

Ain't Misbehavin'
Ain't She Sweet?
Baby Face
The Man I Love

My Blue Heaven
Side By Side
Spread A Little Happiness
When You're Smiling

THE THIRTIES
including:

All Of Me
A Fine Romance
I Wanna Be Loved By You
I've Got You Under My Skin

The Lady Is A Tramp
Smoke Gets In Your Eyes
Summertime
Walkin' My Baby Back Home

THE FORTIES
including:

Almost Like Being In Love
Don't Get Around Much Any More
How High The Moon
Let There Be Love

Sentimental Journey
Swinging On A Star
Tenderly
You Make Me Feel So Young

THE FIFTIES
including:

All The Way
Cry Me A River
Dream Lover
High Hopes

Magic Moments
Mister Sandman
A Teenager In Love
Whatever Will Be Will Be

THE SIXTIES
including:

Cabaret
Happy Birthday Sweet Sixteen
I'm A Believer
The Loco-motion

My Kind Of Girl
Needles And Pins
There's A Kind Of Hush
Walk On By

THE SEVENTIES
including:

Chanson D'Amour
Hi Ho Silver Lining
I'm Not In Love
Isn't She Lovely

Save Your Kisses For Me
Take Good Care Of My Baby
We've Only Just Begun
You Light Up My Life

THE EIGHTIES
including:

Anything For You
China In Your Hand
Everytime You Go Away
Golden Brown

I Want To Break Free
Karma Chameleon
Nikita
Take My Breath Away

THE NINETIES
including:

Crocodile Shoes
I Swear
A Million Love Songs
The One And Only

Promise Me
Sacrifice
Think Twice
Would I Lie To You?

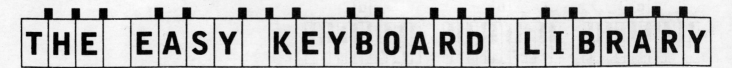

Printed in England
The Panda Group · Haverhill · Suffolk · 8/00